STEPHENIE MEYER

Author of the
TWILIGHT SERIES

by Lori Mortensen

Snap books®

CAPSTONE PRESS
a capstone imprint

Snap Books are published by Capstone Press,
1710 Roe Crest Drive, North Mankato, Minnesota 56003
www.mycapstone.com

Cataloging-in-Publication Data is on file with the Library of Congress.
ISBN 978-1-5157-1329-6 (library binding)
ISBN 978-1-5157-1337-1 (paperback)
ISBN 978-1-5157-1341-8 (eBook PDF)

Editorial Credits

Abby Colich, editor; Bobbi Wyss designer;
Kelly Garvin, media researcher; Laura Manthe, production specialist

Photo Credits

Alamy: Ben Molyneux, 21, The Protected Art Archive, 5; AP: Matt Sayles, 25, Todd
Williamson/Invision for Sony, 29; Corbis/Steven Georges/Press-Telegram, 19; Getty
Images: George Frey, 10; Newscom: David Edwards Image Collection, 28, DVS iPhoto
Inc., 6, Michael Melia/Retna/Photoshot, 26, Richie Buxo/Splash News, 15; Shutterstock:
89 studio, 9 (bottom), 17 (b), 27, Andrey Bayda, 17 (top), dugdax, 4, jaguar PS, 22,
jessicakirsh, 9 (t), Netfalls-Remy Musser, cover, 1, Ollyy, 11, Undrey, 13

Printed in China.
007736

TABLE OF CONTENTS

CHAPTER 1

A Dream Come True

Stephenie Meyer had an unusual dream the night of June 2, 2003. In a sunlit meadow surrounded by a dark forest, a boy and a girl were talking. It was a strange sight. The boy was a beautiful vampire. His skin sparkled in the sun like diamonds. The girl was an ordinary human. They were deeply in love, except there was a teensy problem ...

He was dying to kill her!

It's a vampire thing.

The impossible love story captured Stephenie's imagination. It was a romance doomed to fail, right?

One of the most famous novels about vampires is *Dracula*. Bram Stoker published this story in 1897. The book is so popular that it has never gone out of print. Stephenie had never read this book before writing *Twilight*.

publish—to produce and distribute a book, magazine, newspaper, or any other printed material so that people can buy it

out of print—when new copies of a book title are no longer being printed

VAMPIRE DREAMING

Stephenie wondered why she was dreaming about vampires. She hadn't recently watched any vampire movies. She wasn't reading any books about vampires. This dream seemed to come out of nowhere.

Stephenie woke around 4:00 a.m. She lay in bed trying to remember each detail of the dream before it faded away. But soon enough this stay-at-home mother had to get out of bed. She had a busy day ahead taking care of her three young sons.

WRITING IT ALL DOWN

When Stephenie finally found a moment of free time later in the day, she rushed to her computer. "In the sunlight, he was shocking ..." she began typing.

One page. Two pages. By the end of the day, she had written 10 pages. These pages eventually became Chapter 13 of her first book, *Twilight*. Stephenie didn't set out to write a book. She only wanted to capture the scene from her dream. But when she finished, she couldn't stop wondering what would happen next.

Stephenie Meyer

FROM FIRST BOOK TO BEST SELLER

Three months later Stephenie had finished a 500-page book. It was an amazing feat. She had never written a book of any size before. But it was just a lark, written only for herself. And she was OK with that. No one else would want to read it anyway, she thought.

Stephenie was wrong—big time!

Soon after its 2005 release, sales launched *Twilight* to number 1 on *The New York Times* Best Sellers list. Its **sequels** *New Moon*, *Eclipse*, and *Breaking Dawn* became staples on the list for several years. Later the books became blockbuster movies, earning billions of dollars at the box office.

Stephenie Meyer—an ordinary mom with a dream—became a literary superstar.

> " Once I'd written everything that I'd dreamed, I was eager to know more about what would happen to these intriguing characters. So I kept typing, letting the story go where it wanted to go. "
>
> —Stephenie Meyer interview with Cynsations blog, March 27, 2006

sequel—a story that carries the existing one forward

CHAPTER 2

Passion for Classics

Stephenie Morgan was born on Christmas Eve in Hartford, Connecticut, in 1973. Her parents named her after her father, Stephen, by adding an "ie" to the end of his name. When she was 4, her family moved to Phoenix, Arizona.

Stephenie came from a large family. She often helped take care of her younger siblings. When she wasn't busy being a big sister, she read books—lots of them. By age 8 she was reading novels written for adults. *Gone with the Wind* and *Pride and Prejudice* were on her reading list. Young Stephenie read all types of books—except horror. She was too chicken.

HIGH SCHOOL YEARS

Stephenie was a first-rate student in high school, but she felt like an outsider. There were fancy cars in the student parking lot. Some girls had plastic surgery to enhance their looks. Stephenie didn't put too much thought into her looks. She didn't even have a car.

Stephenie worked hard, and it paid off. She won the **National Merit Scholarship**. She graduated from high school in 1992.

National Merit Scholarship—a special award that comes with money for college given to the top high school students in the country

WHAT'S IN A NAME?

Stephenie chose the names of her main characters in *Twilight* carefully. She named the vampire Edward for the Edwards in two of her favorite books—*Jane Eyre* by Charlotte Brontë and *Sense and Sensibility* by Jane Austen. Stephenie's female character felt as dear to her as her own child. So Stephenie gave her the name she had been saving for if she ever had a daughter, Isabella.

MORE READER THAN WRITER

After high school, Stephenie attended Brigham Young University in Provo, Utah. She majored in English. Stephenie's love for reading led her to focus on literature.

Although Stephenie loved to read, writing was different. "I was terrified of creative writing," said Stephenie. "I did not think the stories I told myself would be interesting to anyone else, and I did not know if I could produce on command."

Stephenie took one writing class in college only because she had to. She chose poetry. She thought she could bluff her way through it.

Stephenie received her degree in English from Brigham Young University in 1997.

A LIFE OF READING

When she was 21, Stephenie married Christian Meyer. He was a friend she had known since childhood. Three years later she graduated from college. Eventually she became the mother to three boys—Gabe, Eli, and Seth. Stephenie spent some of her free time scrapbooking. She made fancy Halloween costumes for her sons. But reading was her true passion. While she cradled a baby in one arm, she held a book in the other. Stephenie often read five or six novels a week.

She had no idea that one night a whole new story would start with one dream.

✔ FACT

Vampire characteristics vary in different stories. The traditional definition of a vampire is "a corpse that rises at night to drink the blood of the living." Often vampires are portrayed with long fangs and a black cape. Stephenie invented her own kind of vampire for *Twilight*.

CHAPTER 3

Dreaming Big

At first Stephenie did not tell anyone she was writing a book about vampires. She thought others would think it sounded cheesy. So without explanation, she dropped out of sight and wrote. No scrapbooking. No going to the movies. No long talks with friends.

But she could not disappear forever. When Stephenie stopped returning phone calls and e-mails, her sister Emily wanted to know why. Stephenie finally spilled the beans. She let her sister read what she had been writing. Emily loved it! As soon as she finished one chapter, Emily would demand to read the next. When Stephenie finally finished writing, Emily urged her to get the book published.

PUBLISHING FEARS

Stephenie didn't know anything about publishing a book. She began doing online research to learn about the process. Stephenie found everything very overwhelming.

Submitting something she'd worked so hard on was scary. It felt like turning her baby over to a stranger. What if they rejected it? Stephenie almost called it quits.

> " The whole set up ... was extremely intimidating, and I almost quit there. It certainly wasn't belief in my fabulous talent that made me push forward; I think it was just that I loved my characters so much, and they were so real to me, that I wanted other people to know them, too. "
>
> —Stephenie Meyer blog entry, October 5, 2005

STARTING THE PROCESS

Stephenie sent about 15 **queries** to small **literary agencies** and **publishing houses**. Several sent her rejections. Some didn't answer at all. Stephenie's younger sister Heidi told her about Janet Evanovich's website. Janet Evanovich is the successful author of several novels. On her website Janet calls the literary agency Writers House "the real thing." So Stephenie included Writers House when sending out queries. She thought such a major agency would be the least likely to respond.

Stephenie was wrong. An assistant at Writers House asked to see the first three chapters of her book. Stephenie was nervous. She didn't think that the first three chapters were the story's strongest part. A few weeks later, however, the assistant asked to see the entire manuscript. And a month after that, Stephenie got a phone call. An **agent** at Writers House wanted to represent her book!

query—a letter sent asking for information or a response
literary agency—a business that acts on behalf of writers
publishing house—a company that publishes books and magazines
agent—someone who helps a writer find a publisher

Janet Evanovich has written more than 60 romance and mystery novels for adults.

✔ FACT

Stephenie originally called her book *Forks*. This is the name of the town where the story takes place. She and her agent changed it to *Twilight* before submitting the manuscript to publishers.

CLOSING THE DEAL

Before they submitted it to publishers, Stephenie and her agent revised and polished the manuscript. Soon nine editors were interested. Little, Brown and Company, a major publisher in New York, expressed the most interest. They offered an **advance** of $300,000 for Stephenie's manuscript and two sequels. It was a staggering offer. New authors usually only receive a few thousand dollars as an advance. Publishers don't want to spend a lot of money on a book before they're sure it will sell well. This offer showed that Little, Brown thought *Twilight* would be big.

To Stephenie's horror, her agent turned down the offer. Stephenie nearly threw up.

Instead, the agent asked for a $1 million advance.

Little, Brown made a **counteroffer** of $750,000. It was the most money they had ever offered to a first-time author.

advance—a payment given prior to work being completed
counteroffer—an offer made in response to an initial offer

Hachette Book Group is located on Avenue of the Americas in New York City.

BIG CITY PUBLISHING

Most of the largest book publishing companies in the United States are located in New York City. Many authors aspire to be published by one of the "Big Five"—Hachette Book Group, HarperCollins, Macmillan, Penguin Random House, and Simon & Schuster. Stephenie's publisher, Little, Brown, is part of Hachette.

CHAPTER 4

Publishing Success

Little, Brown released *Twilight* in 2005. "It was the combination of desire and danger that drew me in," recalled Megan Tingley, the Little, Brown editor who accepted the manuscript. "On a gut level I knew I had a best seller on my hands when I was halfway through the manuscript."

Tingley was right.

In addition to reaching number 1 on *The New York Times* Best Sellers list, the magazine *Publishers Weekly* named *Twilight* one of the best children's books of 2005. The book remained a top seller for years. It was 2008's biggest selling title.

> I was incredibly ... lucky with the publishing process. I wrote *Twilight* over the summer of 2003. I didn't think about publishing at all until it was entirely done—I was just telling myself a story. Writing just for the sake of writing, just for my own pleasure, was certainly the greatest highlight of the whole experience.
>
> —Stephenie Meyer interview with Cynsations blog, March 27, 2006

The Twilight series has sold more than 120 million copies worldwide and was translated into 38 languages.

WRITING THE SEQUELS

Stephenie had written *Twilight* with ease. Thinking that no one would ever read her story, she didn't put any pressure on herself to write something great. Writing the sequels was different. Now millions of eyes were waiting to pounce on every word. Stephenie found this challenging. Eventually, though, she got into a new groove. She wrote three more titles for the series.

In 2006 Little, Brown released *New Moon*, the second book in the series. It spent more than 25 weeks at number 1 on *The New York Times* Best Sellers list. The novel became a global **phenomenon**. Fans celebrated with midnight parties and vampire-themed proms. During the next two years, Stephenie finished *Eclipse* and *Breaking Dawn*. *Breaking Dawn* broke records by selling 1.3 million copies in the United States in the first 24 hours.

✔ FACT

Stephenie writes to music. Her favorite artists include Muse, Linkin Park, My Chemical Romance, Coldplay, The All American Rejects, Travis, Brand New, U2, Jimmy Eat World, and Weezer.

phenomenon—a very unusual or remarkable event

BOOK LEAK

In 2008 Stephenie began writing a new book, *Midnight Sun*. Then 12 chapters of the rough draft were leaked on the Internet. The novel was to be *Twilight* retold from Edward's perspective. After the leak Stephenie decided to stop working on the novel indefinitely. She thought that the unauthorized release of the manuscript would influence her writing too much.

Robert Pattinson and Kristen Stewart starred in the movie versions of the Twilight books.

HITTING HOLLYWOOD

In 2008 *Twilight* hit the big screen. Stephenie was thrilled with the cast. She was able to make suggestions during production. One change she requested was to tone down a kissing scene between Edward and Bella. Stephenie thought it was too much too soon. Their relationship needed to deepen over time. The director agreed. He reshot the scene.

Although Stephenie was involved with the production, she had no idea how the final product would turn out. When it was time to see a **rough cut**, Stephenie was terrified. If the movie was horrible, she would be heartbroken. Stephenie came prepared to make a list of everything she wanted to change. By the end, however, she had not written a word. It was everything she had hoped it would be.

The remaining movies in the Twilight saga—*New Moon, Eclipse, Breaking Dawn Part 1,* and *Breaking Dawn Part 2*—hit theaters over the next four years. All five films grossed billions of dollars worldwide, cementing the franchise's place in history.

✔ FACT

Stephenie has a **cameo** in the *Twilight* movie. At a restaurant before the camera focuses on Bella and her father, a waitress serves a veggie plate to a woman at the counter. That woman is Stephenie!

rough cut—an edited, yet not final, version of a film

cameo—a brief appearance by a celebrity

CHAPTER 5

Twilight and Beyond

Since *Twilight*'s phenomenal success, a lot has changed. Stephenie has made appearances around the world. She has talked with thousands of fans and signed countless autographs. She enjoys meeting her fans. Stephenie says that if you are not writing for teenage girls, you are missing a lot of love.

But not everything has changed. Stephenie has not let the hoopla surrounding her books go to her head. She prefers to be at home rather than anywhere else.

Stephenie continues to write, balancing her time with her family. "I mostly write at night, from eight—when my kids go to bed—till whenever I am close to passing out from exhaustion," said Stephenie. "I edit sometimes during the day, but the words never really flow the same when I am being constantly interrupted."

> I think that after 30 years of being the most normal person in the whole world, it's really hard to become ungrounded. When I'm not out on tour or doing photo shoots, I tend to just forget about it all.
>
> —Stephenie Meyer interview with *USA Today*, July 30, 2008

Stephenie takes a selfie with a fan at the Eclipse movie premier.

OTHER WRITING

Before the release of *Breaking Dawn*, Stephenie published a novel for adults. *The Host* is a **paranormal** romance between a body-snatching alien and her boyfriend. Stephenie got the idea during a long drive between Phoenix and Salt Lake City. To fill the time, she told herself a story. It wasn't long before she knew she'd latched onto another winning story line. With the success of the Twilight series behind her, *The Host* debuted at number 1 on *The New York Times* Best Sellers list. Stephenie was thrilled to prove she wasn't "just a vampire girl."

The Host *became a film in 2013.*

A BOOK FOR CHARITY

In 2010 Stephenie released *The Short Second Life of Bree Tanner*. This **novella** tells the story of Bree, whom readers first met as a newborn vampire in *Eclipse*. Stephenie donated $1.5 million of proceeds from the book to the American Red Cross. "It's amazing to have the opportunity to help those so greatly in need," Stephenie said.

paranormal—a genre of writing that deals with topics that can't be explained by science

novella—a work of fiction longer than a short story but shorter than a novel

WRITING PROCESS

Stephenie has an unusual writing process. She starts with the most exciting scenes first. Then she builds more scenes from those. When each section is finished, she finds ways to tie them together. She likes this process. As she stitches scenes together, it picks up speed like a train zooming down the tracks until it reaches its final destination—the end of the story.

Stephenie at a book signing for Life and Death

FUTURE PROJECTS

In 2013 Stephenie produced the movie *Austenland*. It is a romantic comedy that reconnected her with beloved classic Jane Austen literature.

Stephenie announced another new novel in 2015 for the 10th anniversary of *Twilight*. *Life and Death: Twilight Reimagined* is the *Twilight* story retold with the male and females roles reversed. Beau is a teenage boy in love with a vampire girl named Edythe.

No doubt, Stephenie has many new projects on the horizon. But whether they are sparked by a dream, a long stretch of road, or her love of classic literature, Stephenie is not just waiting around. She does not have the time. She's too busy living her dream.

Stephenie with the director and writer of Austenland

Glossary

advance (ad-VANSS)—a payment given prior to work being completed

agent (AY-juhnt)—someone who helps a writer find a publisher

cameo (KA-me-yoh)—a brief appearance by a celebrity

counteroffer (KAUN-tuhr-OFF-uhr)—an offer made in response to an initial offer

literary agency (LIT-uhr-air-ee AY-juhn-see)—a business that acts on behalf of writers

National Merit Scholarship (NASH-uh-nuhl mare-ET SKOL-ur-ship)—a special award that comes with money for college given to the top high school students in the country

novella (NO-vehl-uh)—a work of fiction longer than a short story but shorter than a novel

out of print (OUT OF PRINT)—when new copies of a book title are no longer being printed

paranormal (pair-uh-NOR-muhl)—a genre of writing that deals with topics that can't be explained by science

phenomenon (fe-NOM-uh-non)—a very unusual or remarkable event

publish (PUHB-lish)—to produce and distribute a book, magazine, newspaper, or any other printed material so that people can buy it

publishing house (PUHB-lish-eeng HOWSE)—a company that publishes books and magazines

query (KWARE-ee)—a letter sent asking for information or a response

rough cut (RUHF CUT)—an edited, yet not final, version of a film

sequel (SEE-kwel)—a story that carries the existing one forward

Read More

Guillain, Charlotte. *What Is a Novel?* Connect with Text. Chicago: Heinemann Raintree, 2015.

Owen, Ruth. *Vampires and Other Bloodsuckers.* Not Near Normal: The Paranormal. New York: Bearport Publishing, 2013.

Scherer, Lauri S. *Stephenie Meyer.* People in the News. Detroit: Lucent Books, 2012.

Internet Sites

FactHound offers a safe, fun way to find Internet sites related to this book. All of the sites on FactHound have been researched by our staff.

Here's all you do:

Visit *www.facthound.com*

Type in this code: 9781515713296

Super-cool stuff!

Check out projects, games and lots more at **www.capstonekids.com**

Critical Thinking Using the Common Core

1. Where did Stephenie Meyer get the idea for the Twilight series? (Key Idea and Details)

2. What if Stephenie's sister had not pushed her to get *Twilight* published? Do you think she ever would have tried to get her book published? Explain why or why not. (Integration of Knowledge and Ideas)

3. Reread the text on page 24 and look at the photo on page 25. What feelings do you think Stephenie had while this photo was being taken? (Craft and Structure)

Index